I can't work when I get high
Everything comes out wrong
Each word I write feels like a lie
I sing and it sounds like somebody else's song.
I sing like Tool, not Tim.
I play like Flea, not me.
I love like love in the movies.
I lie like it's a role on TV.

Cherry blossom rose petals, my meaningless things
Wash away quickly as the hummingbird sings
And follows me down the path of High Sierra's spring.
Listen so closely you may hear it's wings
Follow me kindly I want you in fling
For touch is all I know, beyond meaningless things.
Wallow here with me my rose petal queen
Live with me gently we'll welcome new Spring
Keep me here, tame me, make me grow new wings
And I'll learn to live without meaningless things.
A crutch, put it kindly, you hate when I sing
I hate to stay in one place, addicted to a new ring
It's my mountain of metal, I declare myself king
Then I'll drown tomorrow, in my meaningless things.

Sometimes I wish for winter
For a moment alone to pray
Maybe the silence and the stillness
Could combat this oppressive summer's day.
Sometimes I wish for rain to fall
To soak my hair and splash my skin
Maybe the rain could lift me up
Into a sky where I could see you grin.
You got me through winter
Through all my coldest and frozen days
You pushed me back towards the sunlight
To bask in the sun's new rays.
You got me through the winter
But if I might have my say
I'll stay in this sunlight forever
And summer too, might decide to stay.

Joy is birthing sadness
Like freedom leads to jail
I got into Western
And you got into Yale
This blackness knows no boundaries
Tows no fine class line
You killed yourself for your prestige
I'll need to keep you alive for mine.
Manipulator, micromanager, perpetrator
Leave me be tonight
This blackness knows no boundaries
I lie awake with thoughts of you, tonight.
So boil me in water I'll save you from sun
Leave me here to wither I'll make sure you had fun
Because I needed you when you weren't there
I needed the heart that left with a tear
I needed you
And the blackness made that unclear.

It's 8 in the morning

I have work in an hour

I haven't slept yet

The milk in the fridge has gone sour

I'd focus if I could think

And I'll think when I'm dying

Of you under new moon

When you stopped me from crying.

So now I'll come closer

I want to know if you think I'm clever

We'll be alone

Solitude for us forever, seems kind.

Since that day you never left, my mind.

It's nearing midnight

I sleep with another

She's you, but she's older

I'm me, I've grown colder, in my mind.

Solitude forever, seems kind.

Old man, you poet of poetry's better days
Old man, you scold me when you talk of better ways
Boxed in. I see, there's a greater star above
Conforming. I'm stuck, inside of your nostalgic love.
You see grey's in great colors where I see a cloudy haze
I saw new ways towards others, you set my path ablaze
But old men get older when they deny the younger ways
Old men get colder when they decide to turn away.
Old man, you speak like you spoke so well before
Old man goes on and on about another long lost war
Old man turns back in his mic, they don't love him anymore
When an old man chooses to listen, aging backwards
Looking forth.

You sound like rocks under water
You feel like steam on my face
You look like curiosity uncovered
You still freeze me in my place.
I can't force myself to work no more
I can't focus on a task
I can't pretend it doesn't hurt no more
I'm locked in place and you're my cast.
But our river's flown high
And our river's flown old
Carved through mountains over time
It cuts closer to the bone.
Now our river might go dry
You have left it all alone
Sometimes the river makes me cry
This love could've been my home.
There's sand on the river's bed
It gets all between my toes
Water's rapid near the river's head
Sometimes I wade in with the cold.
Remember skipping rocks with me
Remember days of old
Remember our river's highest points
Remember growing old.
Now our river might go dry
You have left it all alone
Sometimes the river makes me cry
This love could've been my home.

Silence followed silence

Which followed painfully dead air

Phoebe scanned my poems

Soon her face turned into deep despair.

I spoke of her kindly, I called her out by name

I called out for her in the moments, of my deepest of pain

My pen was my tell-all, she opened up my book

Phoebe answered no calls

I could tell from just one look.

She built her sanctum of borrowed guidance

Phoebe Green and the mind of a crook

She had borrowed at my limits of vibrance

Phoebe Green and ambitious overlook

Phoebe pale in invisibility's violence

Phoebe's blank and senseless surprise. Phoebe took.

Cry before the children
Maybe they'll learn how to cry out for love
Kneel below them
Maybe they'll learn the perspective of a dove.
I was taught from the flowers
I was taught from the books
Ego of another brought me into this world
Humility has taught me new ways to look.
Sit the children down in silence
Listen to the wind through the trees
Listen to rivers flowing over stones
Think of others before you think of me.

Sometimes I find myself desperate, unsure
Looking for something to believe in a world impure
I look to the clouds and I close my eyes
Will I learn of God's love when I mature?
I've got a hard time figuring who I should trust
Whether intuition is heavenly
Or I'm in my head too much.
But I know I believe in new sun's light
I believe in the magic of the night
And no matter how hard I fall
I believe that each day is a day I could get it right.

We run back to the places we're comfortable
You to the others
Me, my new friends.
The weeks and the months spent retreating together
I carry them with me
Until my loving end.
We flew, high, deep 'til the pressure could kill
Neck deep, then dive in just for your thrill
Be here, that smile is worth water's chill
To me, your love is the top of my hill
Be my thrill.
We keep an arms distance, avoiding attraction
My head remains forward
You look at your feet.
We stay out of orbit, fearing connection
You keep me alone at night
I took your heat.
We flew, high, deep 'til the pressure could kill
Neck deep, then dive in just for your thrill
Be here, that smile is worth water's chill
To me, your love is the top of my hill
Let's be still.
Please just keep running
Your drama, you're acting
Leave me in trauma
I'm selfish, I'm gasping
Just keep me away from this loving thing
Interiorism allows me to hide.

Shed your clothes softly not to interrupt
The people down singing they just don't know what
They are missing, when they sing on nights so alone
Upstairs, don't upset them, just leave them alone.
Keep looking to me, my one smiling muse
Upstairs is safety, I find comfort in you.
For once I was a singer, downstairs with the crew
Rambling and gambling
The desperation of man
Now the attic's repurposed
For lovers again.
I saw Jordy, saw Mathis, saw Jim coming in
They all shook hands with these skin level grins
But when I took the stairs, their faces did sour
Loneliness finds company in those without power.
Mathis, he grabbed my arm, asked me to sing
I told him I was off, to more primal things
I spoke of the attic and of love's eternal spring.
I spoke to him gently I spoke with no pride
I spoke to him softly, said there'll come a time.

See you again, I'm falling behind
Run you around, I can't much longer hide
Fall with me slowly, my Chelsea goodbye
King me, I'm dying, to keep you alive
Keep me from falling behind.
Run and step softly, my morning sun's high
Light me up, gently, never say goodbye
Keep me up all night, stare into my eye
Create your own world, let me live in your mind
Please keep me from falling behind.
You dress me up, to take me out, to spend quality time
You keep me there, talk to me, make me feel I am kind
This light above, it draws me near, you keep me aligned
But don't let me keep falling behind.

In October, its darker, it feels like we're all leaving soon

The moon is out,

It's looking like,

October's extending towards June

Since you called me under moonlight and said you're coming soon

October's night has invaded June.

Green leaves, they start falling, from summer night's sky

You lead me to my calling,

But now I won't see July,

If this night could last long past due

October's night has invaded June.

Knowing leaves crumble, the sky has turned black

Trick or treat quietly we don't want to go back

All these summer nights are ending too soon

You lay with me

Staring into the light of the moon

You kiss me

Tell me your leaving at noon

But October's night has invaded June.

On the day that my mother went free

She didn't do what they said that she'd done to me

She was a woman alone, her guitar, and her glee

Loving one man and being scorned by he

On the day my mother went free.

On the day that my father left me

He spat at my mother before spitting at me

He called to his daughter, he killed sweet Louise

On the day that my father left me.

My mother, the body, confusion of love

She opened the attic, hid her above

Gave me a hug and told me to run

My mother's confusion of love.

My mother, the sirens, she headed the call

My mother, the killer

My mother, she's gone

On the day she became a pawn.

Leave me alone, this house has grown on

Keep me away, I see my father and hide

I wait for the day, wait silently

For the day that my mother goes free.

I'm growing old with nothing to say
Like a fragile brown leaf on a long winter's day
Sickness and time, they've taken my voice
In sickness, I rhyme, I no longer have a choice.
I use my final gasps to sing out
One last song, in hope or en route
In search of a voice that forgets youthful doubt.
Something to pass long after my time has come
Something to live, after sickness has won
I want to die but I want to be free
In ideas, in art, in my life's melancholy
I know it's my time to be with old friends
But sing my song sometime, and I'll come again.

Bargain store barbicide
My head is filled with cyanide
Your voice sounds like a diatribe
Your eyes light up like fireflies.
I'm fortunate in servitude, I just like to look at you
Call me when you're in the mood
Borrow me I feel unused.
Kiss my chest I'll kiss your mouth
I'll sleep until you kick me out
I'll stay until you express doubt
Love until the love runs out.
We breath the same lonely air
When we walk we walk as a pair
When you leave I know you were here
That's enough for me.
Calling friends as distraction
Party feels like a lack of passion
People offer no real interaction
Specific eyes specific satisfaction.
Buried in my unsaid words
Buried with the days I slept on curbs
Buried, buried, locked away
Laying with the right words to say.
Creeping slowly to a mortal man
Sleeping too long with only my two hands
Helping no one but myself
This is where the heart goes South.
We breath the same lonely air
When we walk we walk as a pair
When you leave I know you were here
That's enough for me. I swear.

A poet's tongue is behind closed lips

Hidden in movements as it mimics observations of the outside world

It channels the energy into fingers and writing

Gathers all that is necessary to achieve the inspiring.

Old friends live in the passing tides

They seem to slow down as I watch them pass by

They smile in the reflections from the sun

And they drift along

A river isn't a river if it ends it's run.

All coffee no water

All French toast no fruit

I'm sustained by my father

I'm fed by the passions of refute.

Like the grand scheme of a grandfather

Like the strength to pick you up

Like looking into depending eyes of love

I feel whole when I'm most stuck.

There's stillness in the air, our bodys have gone cold

Motionless, I stare

Bleeding hearts, we are not bold.

There's a sun shining through the dark, pierced into my room

You sit up in your mark

I stare directly into my doom.

All the myths we believed, all the lies we forget

I see the unseen

I stayed silent while you wept.

Our father's forgive us, for we are still young

There's too much space between us

Our web's been silently spun.

Not to say I lack the hope

I've never lacked the will to try

Not to say that I cannot cope

If you leave I will not cry

All I can say is all that I know

And I know that I hate to pry

But what if I asked to start over again

What if we shed that disguise

What if I ran my finger along your brow

What if we killed these mutual lies.

Walking across Walker St.

My red rain jacket hung to my feet

My cross to bare was too much for me

Yellow light drowned on Walker St.

I've been killing myself in hopes that I'd come free

I'd been walking so long that my heart sunk to my knees

I could live forever if I could only live with me

I could get so much better if I could leave Walker St.

I stare into eyes that question me back

As I question them I'm sure

They wonder so much as blank canvas walks by

To them I must seem so pure

But I feel dirty, I've traveled too far from my home

Far away from the love of my youth

I have become the moments that live outside of your time

I have become more Walker St. than my own.

Just saying, I tried

You created a world of contraction and walls

I cried in the night when I struggled against my own pitfalls

I could never describe it when the daylight calls

But I had to hide if I wanted to fit.

Just saying, I lied

I lived in a world of self loathing in sin

Pretending that I won't make same mistakes over again

Until they crept back casually and became medicine

I lied and I am bound to lie again.

Just saying, I left

Without a word in my greatest theft

I just couldn't bare the pain in my chest

Alleviated by space and by the unkempt

The walls became a gate and I couldn't be kept.

Just saying, I tried

To hide in your love and pretend you had mine

Inviting enough it seemed for a time

Stagnation and safety they might as well rhyme

But safety went sour

Stagnation grows sour in time.

For those who brood in the fires
Who can't see the scar that's left
For those who hide their desires
As they burn too low to see the real theft
They burn you in their lonely frustration
They burn you when you want your own time
They hold you in some righteous indignation
They cast you out long before your time.
For those who walk on tightrope elation
No net for catching the fall
For those who create out of God's creation
This is for those who stop when you call.
They fall from grace that's hidden in revelation
They fall in the dark of self mythology
They catch the spirit of spritely resignation
They fall apart when a tear comes to the seams.

I never considered the road between homes as a gateway
I never stopped along the dotted yellow lines
I never considered how the places between
Could be my capsules away from my limited time
I never stopped to smell the flowers
And the slight scented differences between
A flower was always just a flower
Until I acknowledged the totality of the scene
I never opened the door when the rain came down
I never liked the smell of wet cement
Any excuse to lock in and tune out
Any way I could avoid getting drenched
Now I see the water's a gift
A prize of survival for the flower
Now I see the flower's scent
I can afford to stop
I can afford to spend another hour.

I'm distracted by the remnants of voices that pass behind the back of my mind

Contracted to the world around me they seem as real as you and I

I can't feel the rain on my skin, I'm too busy with you on my mind

Disconnected from my thoughts within

I'm no more my skin than the sky.

My brother was a martyr, unafraid of the light of day

My brother was a fighter until the day his mark got made

My brother's in the ground we never figured why

Now his skin is my skin

And I find him in the sky.

This God must be greater
Than the one I met yesterday
The light of your savior's shining
Brighter upon me today
When she gathered the light of the sun in her arms
Her display
She cracked all the rivers with a stomp of her feet
Now I lay
This God is smiling the winds are all dancing
Along the rivers they play
There's eternal sunshine beyond the clouds
But they broke just for me
Today.
This God likes to savor
The brightest parts of the day
No hurry towards midnight
No sunset fireworks display
This God is a giver
God of nature, God of play
I wish relation for the moment to extend
Beyond the light of this day.

I am the crow with no desire to caw
I am the cuckoo on the other side of your lawn
I am the lone star in Arabian skies
I am the jester
The clown that cries.
I creep through dark alleyways
I creep through the night
I'm aimless in my darkest pursuits
It brings me no delight
This is the dance of the jester.
I bark up the wrong tree over again
I feel what can't feel me, I live in pretend
I borrowed this life from some other within
Jester's makeup is skin deep
See beyond your sanctimony
Inevitability of sin.

My hometown breeds a need for the inbetweens

A dreamlike city's fervor

Disdain for the concept of time

My hometown provides just enough of the little white lies

It told me the world was open

That I could dance along that line

I could borrow, I could share, I could have everything my way

I never cried until I finally moved away

I peered into both sides, played the middle until I left

Safe in mythological options

Outside of my box, I wept

My worldly illusion, referring to all my favorite texts

This town of the careful forgotten

This town of pretentious inept.

You walk around the town you feel least alone in
Stone people call to you, recalling the time you dipped your toe in
But you walk so dignified since you last cried
And you balance on the walls that they stabilized.
You crept around sunny Slavic towns
You kept me arms length away
You flew into that Frenchman's room
You lied in his bed never praised
Now stone people call "you can't destroy what is made"
They cry in the night through your walls made of clay
And you cannot blame them, Mrs. Grenade
Stuck in a sweet memory's parade.
Like vocal chords in your mind you can't escape stone's serenade
So you run back to me for the first time I recall
Flower child seeks freedom in livelihoods of play
The baby first sees them now even baby wants his pay
Stone's screaming won't leave them, flower children are prey
Stone's screaming, it echoes through Mrs. Grenade
She begs me, I can't hear beyond the parade
She kissed me, the lips of the stoneman's decay
She lifts me, we'll live with the screaming each day.

It's eleven thirty-ish

Camp will get hot soon

My belly's full of Ginsberg's Kaddish

But my heart cries out for food

My cantine's filled with coffee

Bitter like the sight of you

Blue skies wash away with strong breezes

They can't wash away what's true.

The Beats are all old now

Shakespear died long ago

They went gently along into what they raged so fiercely against

Some went long before it was there time to go

I went to the City Lights bookstore

I paced through Kerouac's street

Something inside me searched for a beating heart

I searched for the soul of someone I could never meet

Dylan Thomas raged against goodnight

Nobody rages anymore

Sometimes it feels like I tiptoe in catacombs

Life's end becomes monotony

And I refuse to bore.

It gets me down sometimes

I think of Ginsberg's grave

How Ferlingetti peacefully rests

Sometimes I feel like they've been betrayed

Those who try and fail to combat death

Until I think of words on paper

And of rhymes that others wrote

Kerouac's street lights a fire

It's in the moments before each becomes a liar, before we board eternity's boat

I woke up to hear that the world was ending and I wanted to write a poem
Something to encase in space glass that shoots into the atmosphere
Something to last longer than my time here.
They told me the world was catching fire, they said
"The bleeding heart's failure is clear"
They arrested the man who broke the news to the rest of us
But they can't make his words disappear
They chided the men that resented us
But everyone needs a career.
I woke up to hear that the world was ending and I wanted to go outside
They said it was burning, I felt the rain
I felt present in the face of my fear.
The fire started one day when I was on a plane
I was flying to see you, spend our final days
I stared down at the fire, I still felt the same
I woke up to hear that the world was ending and I wanted to write you a poem.

All my ex's girlfriends are originally from California
They skate, they surf, they tan
All my ex's girlfriends live in Saratoga
They've got river access, that's cool.
All my ex's girlfriends play rock & roll in rock & roll bands
I took piano lessons when I was a kid
All my ex's girlfriends have been to San Francisco
I wish I did.
My sunburnt arms would lose in arm wrestling
My fiery hair would glow in California sun
My rivers are the sewers and the broken bathtub
My ex's girlfriends seem like lots of fun
Sometimes I feel like staying quiet
Maybe I'm listening for them to sing
Some nostalgic view of my past's future
Cyclical, their voices are like an eternity spring
Sometimes I sit on my back porch
And think about meeting them someday
Like what if we were all in one room
What if they ambushed me on Sunday?
Kill me with their cool-ness
They'd maim me with pretty smiles
But my Sunday ran so normally
Maybe they see me
Intimidation, immaculate style.

Why can't God be the sun

Why can't the rain be her tears

Why can't sunny days shine on everyone

Why did she give me all these fears?

Why wasn't I born as a blackbird in nighttime

Something born to disappear

What made me smart enough to see the pain you caused

Why did she choose to put me here?

I remember my sins like they tattooed on my eyelids

They remind me that sleep is made from fear

I believe in believing in karma

But my bad deed imprintation prints too clear.

The wind flies in my face
The sunlight's shining through
You tell me the truth is in patience and grace
Do I look like Jesus to you?
I looked across the valley
Sharp rocks they lined it's floor
You disappeared from our spots in the alleys
You don't want me to find you anymore?
Everyday I feel getting older
Sometimes I wake up in pain
Like Sisyphus pushing his boulder
What if one day I can't find my restraint?
I'm leaning out your window
While you listen to Bitches Brew
You tell me you need me to understand
Do I look like Jesus to you?

You and I moving, parallel movements
We dance side by side, we never touch
You and I moving, parallel movements
Sometimes I lean close to whisper, never too much
You and I moving, parallel movements
The clock on the wall is frozen in moments
You and I moving, parallel movements
It broke the last time we tried to stop time
You and I moving, parallel movements
These moments of echo have burned in my mind
Each time they lost volume, I'm losing touch
Each time they seem hollower, I'm thinking too much
Each time I think I'm right, to learn I have so much
You and I moving, parallel movements
We'll walk side by side, never to clutch.

There's blood on the pavement outside my locked door
It's the proper treatment for the lives that I knew before
For the lives that struggled against the onslaught breeze
The lives that hardened when they turned away from me
There's people that gather outside every day
They put up their banners
I listen when they pray
There's people that gather outside my locked door
It's a funeral procession each year to the day
It's a market correction facilitated by those who can't pay
And it's my gravestone that they've made out of clay.
Unlocked, I'm a liar, exposed in the outside sun
They'll all leave so uninspired, I'm not the greatest undead son
Unlocked, I'm a liar, riddled with the outside's guilt
They can't know that I perspire, protect this house of cards I've built.

I'll agree to drive you as long as you let the music play
I'll walk like we used to every night next to Bellingham Bay
I'll sing you a song as long as you don't sing one back
I'll write you a poem as long as you promise not to laugh
I'll sit with you quietly we can look at the sea
I could tell you how this darkness inspires me if you agree that you'll leave
I could give you a present as long as you agree not to cry
We can share this life as long as you promise to ignore me when I walk by.
We can talk about the present, never anything more
Not about how you gave me away once before
Not about how you sold my songs to a man
With a pick in his teeth and a guitar in his hand
Not about how you changed the eye of your stare
To a far freer face and the drummer in my band
Not about my past or how it seeps into tonight
Not about what happens when you turn off your light
Not about family, not about what happened to our time
We can remain friends forever
As long as you keep me blind.

Such a smile on her face

It's such a meaningful embrace

Calm and collected, she takes in the neglected

She's gold and free and loud

Should I mention Miss Good Intentions next time she comes around?

Such an overdue goodbye

It took me so long to get caught in my lie

Give me some meaning, she's got a need for healing

And I'll give her all of my time

Should I mention Miss Good Intentions next time she calls the house?

She put flowers in my hair

It's such a good feeling behind both of my ears

I feel like I'm teething, in my search for deeper meaning

And I'm retracing all of my fears

Should I mention Miss Good Intentions next time you end up in tears?

Such a dreamlike point of view

It's such a foggy haze I thought I saw you

Calm and collected, she takes in the neglected

She's rosy in the morning dew

Should I mention Miss Good Intentions next time I ask for you?

One day you'll tire of the things that excited you before
You'll depress when you forget that old feeling
I know that I know nothing except for one useful pleading

Your life will be long
Your life will have meaning.

Even compilations of nothing, you work to the bone
We could keep searching forever, to end up all alone
Hold onto peaceful moments
Encase every tear
You're living life in performance
Your only audience is already here
It's not usually a bomb
Sometimes it's not really so fleeting

Your life will be long
Your life will have meaning.
I promise.

I find love in the ash that embedded itself in my fingertips
It feels like a petrification of better times
I hope the scent remains until the day I die
Until I'm older
Until I'm truly desperate
Arriving early for Wednesday meetings
At the elderly person's singles club
Constantly smelling my fingers
Reminiscing on memories of better times
Before the elderly person's singles club
Times when my cigarettes weren't deadly
When I still thought that I could sing
Back when the flowers bloomed just for me
You got to town in the Spring.
I think that I've aged rapidly
The smoke has left the air
Now I sit alone waiting to see who's skipping Wednesday prayers
At the elderly person's singles club.
I don't remember my first meeting anymore
I hide when I see my old friends walking through that door
Sometimes I think they'd recognize me
Then I catch a glimpse in my hideout's mirror
At the elderly person's singles club
I've realized my darkest fears
I've been hiding out at the elderly person's singles club for so long
That I've started to belong here.

So strange to live in your head
I can't find consciousness in my hands
Sometimes there's a heart in my stomach
There's revolution in asking for what's there.
So strange to be trapped in my perceptions
Such freedom to live in another
I pray that my eyes won't play tricks on me
Next time I look into the eyes of a lover.
So strange to walk around the buried
Only seeing life teeming above the ground
It's such a cycle that it's almost appealing
I can almost rationalize being bound for the ground.
So strange that this river reminds me of a ticking clock
The water beats against the rocks like I have somewhere to be
Then I watch the river until I realize that the river's never going to stop
And I can finally hear that the ticking clock's inside of me.

Poster children for the human condition

Anne Lamott's family pictures

The flashing time capsule s to freeze our times

"Cheese" is a code word for "Mask what's inside."

God forbid you're crying

God forbid you to frown

You're even hiding from these future versions of you

In case they want to embellish what it was deep down.

Poster children for the practicing

The smiling, the stance, and the stare

The playwright's gone teaching

The singer's gone silent

Poster children pictures in grayscale

God forbidding their vibrance.

I woke up this morning trapped in today
I woke up this morning's dreams felt like yesterday
And somehow my dreams feel like they're decades away.
I woke up this morning trapped in my bed
I thought I heard voices but they were just memories in my head
I thought saw some sympathy rising for the dead
Until I met the man whose face burned scarlet red.
He mentioned things I had always forgotten to say
He asked me about each part of my day
He motioned towards me I got in his car
He freed my mind, now I crave a new start
He exposed my lie, now I crave a new heart.
And though I hate to admit it, the lying was always the best part.

Some prefer to live alone
They don't know the desire to call someone else their own
They borrow the time that others spend
Stuck. Loving skin and bone.
Someone smiled who you didn't know
All the other paths just haven't flown
Before you know it you will show, you're
Stuck. Loving skin and bone.
Search for smaller noises
Learn to love your own
Live for the sake of the roses
Before you find yourself back home
Stuck. Loving skin and bone.

There's mist in between the craggy peaks on my side of the Cascades

The natural greenhouse protects me from the mountainous winter's chill

Ice covered caps stare down at my little brigade

There's screaming behind me, it reminds me what's real.

I trek further through the cover of the wood

The trees, like tents above my head

I keep my head forward, looking towards something good

There's a fire blazing behind me, it reminds me of the times that we bled.

What would escape mean for those left behind me?

What would you have seen inside my eyes?

What would it sound like if I never heard your laughter?

If you never gave your patience

If you never gave your time.

I used my head and I lost belief

The forest's dead, the burning's inside of me

I ran away, I forgot my lines

Thank you for your patience

Thank you for all your time.

I'm contained by my contentment, like the stained glass window that doesn't show
through to the other side
It hides the outside world with distraction, designs to designate you to what is inside
Beauty that dissuades you from looking towards how the other half resides
Contained in your contentment, search beyond your pride.
I'm inspired by my resentment, like the old man who forgets things with his remaining
time
He burns with a young man's passion to recapture his ability to see the signs
Trapped in a child's entanglement, a prison with no life of crime
He fears the fire inside him, he won't be left behind.
I refuse my own repentance, when the children are bleeding yet insisting they're fine
Their smiling faces seek acceptance in a world where blood's a crime
Cartoonishly expressive, they search for disappointment in my eyes
I refuse my own repentance, I will get you off my mind.

My hair's getting longer
I've learned from my lies
My face is looking older
I'm starting to feel wise
Over all this time I've seen no guarantee but surprise
Yet I'm still stuck
Trapped inside my eyes.
My feelings are freer
I've learned from my pain
My skin is getting thicker
As I've moved beyond my shame
Over all this time I've learned the nothingness of tame
Yet I'm still stuck
Trapped inside my brain.
The world could be bigger or it could be just for me
The more it expands the more I'm scared of feeling free
Other people are leading such similar lives
I want them to want to see me.
My life's getting shorter
I'm starting to pray
Abstract somethings above me
Might relieve this malaise
Over all this time I've seen enough to know that there's nothing I can say
But I'm no longer stuck
All I have is today.

I'm recreating the issues that plague the men of our times

I'd recognize the misuse if I could see through these tears in my eyes

And I'd stop to look around if I didn't fear falling behind

I'm too young to hate you

Too old to mind.

The novice is selling his blues

The veteran has run out of time

I'm walking through towns that were never new

I'm running towards some new kind of light.

I'm separating the values that stick one man into his time

I'm starting to look beyond you, noticing all the signs

I'd feel so whole when I saw you, why were you so hard to find

I'm way too young to hate you

I'm way too old to mind.

Thirty years after the nineties I woke up alone
Like Jesus and Mary: Like Stoned and Dethroned
I borrowed a timely word from a woman I'd once known
I carry it with me as I stagger down my throne.
Twenty years post my inception I still haven't found a home
Two decades spent floating: My parents pay my loans
I carry them with me, I try to call on the phone
I open up when I'm home
Until something tries to beseech me, call me when you're alone
So far from living within me, I can't feel my bones.
Ten years after all my innocence spilled
Like wind in sand houses: Like cards that I've built
I'm forgetting my vices and sprinting towards prowess
Like Jesus and Mary: Like facing my cowardice.

I bargained with a storefront man over the dust that fell in his shoe
I started to convince him that I was his man and that I loved someone just like you
He guarded his rust, this old moldy man, his lips just wouldn't spew
I started the rush then I could not stand, I borrowed every trick that you knew
But I came back an empty man
Enlighten me with your blues.
These forces that checked me here, they checked me against my will
They bargained with what I made of my life and they burdened me with cheap thrills
These voices that beckoned my mind soon grew shrill
And I came back an empty man
Protect me from what kills.
I listened to my brother in the nineties
And to Jesus late in life
Still came back an empty man
I've seen what brings the light.

There's a blind bird sitting in the nest next to the table where I write

It chirps into the wind

It hopes to hear something beyond the crackle of my keyboard in return

The bird whispers it's chirp in a voice that's grown husky in it's desperation

It chirps into the wind

The world to the blinded is filled through intimidation.

There's a house upon a hill that I can see from my perch in the backyard of this place

It swarms with the sparrows that can see

They screech in the distance just inaudible to the blind bird and me

They swarm one old lady while her coffee turns to wine

My bird chirps into the wind

Obsessed with something that walks invisibly behind.

There's a market in the city that I watch during the week

There's car keys on the table that allow me to leave

There's places in this world that I would rather be

But I'm stuck at this backyard table

Staring at the bird that is alone in this world

Staring into eyes that can't see me.

You stand there and you worship your God that values
Invisibility over the tangibility of Earthly charity
Secrecy over the olive branch that reaches in daylight and extends a Godly word to
those in need
You stand there, early for the brightest spot of your Sunday. Looking down at me.
I slept through church today so I'm in the mood for questioning over worship
Last week, I needed a prayer for my morning
Last week, I noticed the flies that were buzzing the preacher as he finished his sermon
and when I passed in the hallway, he smelled like gin, like me
Saturday's saint chose being human over heavenly.
There's secrets in those stones
I started going because I thought they were cool buildings
And football's offseason leaves me bored on Sundays
I started going because I thought my life needed reason
Then they told me the secret
Saturday's saint chose a time when I was most unbecoming
They told me the secrets to the walls, they told me simply because I asked
Saturday's saint had been dying to divulge
He even thanked me for scratching at the mask.

Melancholic is the mist that rises against the river's edge
It rises with the sun that peeks over the mountain
My river's done floating, my water's gone to steam
Yet I can't bring my feet away from this dry river's edge.
Melancholic is the mind that spots the sadness of the sea
The disappearing horizon and the waves that are pulling at my feet
I disappear into the distance, I court what I can't see
Yet I can't escape the notion that this time I should be free.
A microwave mind
I don't call
I don't read
Locked away in a million different things
This dry river is all that I need.

A drop of wine fell to her bottom lip. Blended with the dark rose of her lipstick.

She was an artist. From her hair, to her fingers, to her mind.

I was an artist. Scrambling the remnants of what used to be free time.

And I'm built to destroy her. Fine china in her eyes.

She's invisible in the sunlight and blinding in the moon.

And she's built to destroy me. Always built for something new.

She's spoiled and unhappy with the way she looks tonight

She's flowering below me in her hands come powerful light

She's blinding from above me and I sink into her sky

Soon she forgets to love the

Fine china in my eyes.

Thanks for the time and the laughs and the blue
Thank you for coming back home
Time took our the place between the thoughts that we'd spew
Thank you for letting me roam
The bars and the barricades distract from the truth
Like the songs that we sing to remind us of youth
You stopped me from losing my tune
You stopped me from stealing what's true
But this idea of the ideal me
Has carried me far away from you.
It's funny how growth is sometimes a parallel track
I laugh when I think of past yous
New memories will soon turn the old ones to black
Bar-bells, hall crowds, running laps in old shoes
It's funny how many times I've tried to go back
Looking away from the things that are new
Recollection as clamour for the ideals of the past
When the idea of the ideal me
Took me far away from you.

She saved me the waltz
With all the baggage we carry
Three steps in two I had won
She swayed with the waltz
She knew I was married
Her eyes glued to mine in the sun.
She showed me her faults
Stepped over insults
She barked up each tree that I climbed.
She lived for the waltz
Even tears stepped in time
She needed no rhythm
She needed no rhyme.
She saved me the waltz
I showed where you were buried
The years they go by, step in time.

Something turns in the invisible august of my life
Something turns in the distance
Clouds follow me home, they slip me a knife
They'd vanish away from my presence.
Skies are burning to remind you of death
Flames rise in the distance
Orange clouds rise to see what we've lost
While we were trying to fit in
It calls back to the times we bled
It calls to calls unanswered
It stopped me showing scars on my chest
It skipped over something that mattered
Still I caught myself under your dress
Soon I forgot what I gathered.
Late in the summer the skies burn me down
Weather delays the day I thought you'd come down
You can't wait any longer
Next year these skies will burn stronger.

I was born in the darkness of the dirt
Six feet under your foot
Six feet below the death of the surface, six feet below every possible decay
Six feet of space for perspective.
Bred where you will find your end
Comfort in your abstraction
Comfort among the dead
Hell steered away from the satisfaction's pretense.
Hell steered away from the things you don't know
In earthly passion for earthly things
In vibrant flowers next to the hot springs
Hell steered away from parts unknown
Hell steered away from a life of your own.

Empty headed in an empty room. Something that should birth nostalgia.
Furniture, forgotten with memories of you. Nights that we'll never recapture.
I borrowed the lamp that you hated so much
I returned it the day before last
You would've been happy to throw it away
I would've held onto it for another day
To stop you're becoming my past
That lamp made me smile before I shattered the glass.
I'll turn in my keys feeling hollow
I'm moving back home
I'll earn my new keep tomorrow
Soon I will be whole
This empty room
It will become my tomb
This empty room's not home.

My hand hovers over the ripples in your torso

You turn touch into a crutch

Something pulls me closer though I choose to take too much

It's something for those less in touch than us.

Gasping cold air escapes wintery eyes

My lips start to quiver when met with quivering minds

Something to seem less sophisticated than I'm

So I decided to give in, I burn your winter in mine.

Redness in destruction

Smouldering coals

No benevolence in the inaction of

Passively aging souls.

No better narrator than the space between you and I

No better sacrifice to the intimacy of time

No better living than unabashed by lies

No better thrill than those wintery eyes.

Thickening walls that separate the suffering
Strengthening bonds on the day that you lied
Finer things are enjoyed far from my scornful muttering
But you're coughing through the best day of our lives.
Someday we'll look back and smile
Maybe I'll have to look alone
We'll lose our fears for things untitled
Either way I know you shouldn't be alone.
Expanding the space to separate the sickness
We're sleeping in different rooms
They're like bubbles surrounding our parallel lives
I can't bear being buried in your tomb.
Someday things may not be so sour
Making memory of times before
When we were young and I hadn't yet cowered
When the world wasn't steeped in gore.
When the world had no expiration date
When life had so much to assure
When the world offered singularity at that gate
I wasn't always so damn poor
In the days when the world wasn't steeped in gore.

I don't believe in an interventionist God
In revolution divine
In flagrant vocation
I don't believe in any unabashed truths
In dogmatic politicians
In the cardinal sin of youth
But then again, you do
So I question my truth.
I don't believe in the scarcity of love
In the songs your brother sings
In the charity of debutants
I don't believe in your favorite shade of blue
In the gentleman's behavior
In the genius of the new
But then again, you do
So I question my truth.

Black dressed tears and rain outside, black umbrellas up to cloud my skies

A favorite dress and style of hair, black lipstick turned pale this year

Your room's still yours it won't empty

The window damp with untouched decay

Indent where you used to lay

Tears from the ceiling, the house expands

Hangers you'll never reach, guitar you'll never play.

The homogeneity of your dresser

And the monotony of your speech

And your life and it's death obsessions

And the black shadows grim reaping on your cheeks

And the lips that stopped wanting to smile for me

And the calls I called that you left for weeks

And the darkness in your poetry

And the clouds you refused to breech

You and your collection of bones

You falling to your knees

And your funeral and all of its flowers

The life surrounding my deceased.

As I age
I recognize the depth of the lakes inside your lies
Mary mother's generations of loosening family ties
Gathering flowers. Black are her funeral eyes
Spreading too thin to police what occupies my mind
Cousin Malcolm's release
Cousin Katy's goodbye.
As I age
I follow the tracks that laid far before my time
Mary mother's a generation of sickly bloodline
She plants her boots in the mud. I step in line
Soon she grows too weak to guess the things on my mind
Cousin Carl's with police
Cousin Joe does hard time.
Mary, Mary, aspirations of peace
Mother Mary of failure's divine
Turning into a slug
Dragging a leech
Mother Mary's trap is identical to mine.

Burnt orange baseball pants wrap my knees and match the sun over my head
It's sinking towards me, biking home, August is the closest month to death
Suffocating sun, the ache of my acne, Summer's borrowing time against the rapidity.
My face stings more than the back that bends and twists it's way through the night
Damp sheets cut me out of sinking moonlight, everything sinks towards my surface
Beckoning night, the throb in my spine, Summer's crying to see something divine.
Sweat beading, it walks over my skin
Swamp animals screaming in the distance
New seasons, struggle to begin
Escape from Summer's chokehold that drives me within.

The pious are searching for something to feel
The blackballed are aching for somewhere to kneel
The gold of your teeth match the gold of her pay
She took me to Tennessee
Now each new life is a day.

The blameless Reagan youth of locked love
The tortured souls wallow in golden mud
The humidity of the Southern sun's rays
She brought me to Texas
Texas loves me today

She took me to her golden grave
She longed for my blackballed embrace
So far removed from yesterday
She fears golden regret
Mind what could never stay.

We're emotionless canvas of painted on love
We torture each other with projections in silence
Romanticizing moments of violence
Mindlessly searching for something golden above
Mindlessly patronizing what makes us numb.

I stare into the glass, empty for reflection of old times, the bars on the windows, the only thing maintaining my old mind.

I block out the bottom of the light fixture outside

Imagining conversation when the voices were so kind.

I am my lover's instincts

I am my mother's mind.

Isolation in the dark room, generations of "sometime", I part from loving company, compulsions of my time.

Guiding fathers hold my hand and leading me outside

Guiding flowers cover my land and wash my lover's bride.

I am my brother's humor

I can be anything with time.

Your tights and your mask and your glued on baret, they stay on in eternity's pictures of
paint.

Your smile and their frown and the light that you take, encapsulates forever, I'll show at
your wake.

Striving for such seriousness

Strive to raise your life's stakes

Green is the color of that fleeting power

Your face is washed with unrealized mistakes.

I truly admire the courage to accept a young life's potential fate. You're brave when your
chin won't quiver, when those boots refuse to shake

But your time arrived in such mild a manner. Your friends still think revolution's at stake.

Young man's prowess

Young man's fate

Young man's fire fluctuates and fades

Into loyalty for their state.

I sat in a park in Seattle with Naima, her golden locks bounced in step like Coltrane
played each strand of her hair
She collapsed into her wooden seat, pale as the headlights on a deer.
Delicate creatures swirled her delicate head, the thinnest of wings to separate a fall to
their death
Delicate Naima in her summertime dress
Delicate Naima only sang in her head.
The two of us calmed as the wings slowed their fluttering, we scanned the ground
across the street
Searching for cigarettes, discarded satiates for something we need.
Delicate wings settled on my flinching finger
Delicate Naima smoked someone's lost stinger.
I stared at the bug, the bug in Seattle, the bug in the park, the bug in Naima and my
troubled hearts
Naima stared too, she stared with more fervor
Delicate Naima the bride
Naima, butterfly destroyer.

Stillness. Empty house of stone that rests on top of the hill

Silence. Broken only by the wind that whistles through the cracks in the windows and in between the gaps of the ancient stone

The strongest house in Dublin. It stands too long for home.

Broken. The glass that crumbled underneath your foot

Stolen. The space is bare of things that could turn our lives for good, I leech along the empty walls, you gather dust in your hood

The strongest house in Dublin. Shakes in the winds from the growing wood.

Cracks under the dark cloud roofing sky

Splits over the lightning of the night

Burns through the black regatta of fading light

The strongest house in Dublin earned its name in the strength of the fight.

Lurid. The scene of the morning of the crimes

Vivid. The sight of the space between you and I

Livid. My mind to see the pain oozing in your eyes

Effusive. The townsfolk who came to empathize with lies

The strongest house in Dublin

Rubble. A weak whistling collection of goodbyes.

While I'm young. Encapsulated inside the fleeting feeling that is the prime of my life
While I'm here. Apart from the world that would see me in my finest light
While I stay. Entranced in the spill of the freedom that makes up for the strife
Clear for the fight.
While on display. The passers, the readers who think I've got nothing to ask
While I'm trapped. The card holding gawkers who drool through their masks
While I run through the tasks that keep me away from participant's laps
While I dive past the kiss and the hands of the crass
Maintain class.
A doubled stray of the misplaced love I crave
A lie the morning after
A phrase of praise from this bed we lay
A time abandoning laugher
You stay
I gray
This leaving's longing to matter.

A tube through the mouth and the nose of my lord
Jaqueline's jealousy wielding its sword
A hole in his throat and beeping life support
Jaqueline's smoke signal staring endures.
Try to paint a scene with a paintbrush of words
Try to make a living while your mind walks on swords
Try to keep me living when God's love won't mature
Alive are the unliving when they fall in love with chores.
And Jaqueline so forgiving, I forget the profundity of my chorus
And my God of holy stealing, inspiring backward search
The start to the new morning, new life in Jaqueline's church.
Found in a piano's lark-like song
In observation of the dirt
Found in guilt staring through the halls
At guidance of gathering hurt
Jaqueline's love untethered, Jaqueline killing for sport.

I remember a time being soft-headed

Top heavy and bobbling my face in the dirt

Hoarding small objects in my pockets of rodent skulls, a piece of your skirt

Keeping pace with the care you let everyone see

Searching for something you'd share just for me.

I remember times of white headed dogs

Hopeful short-lived soul won't notice the hurt

Dirt drenched coat with a red wine smile

Living in love with advice from a child

To gather, to search for dreams in the clouds

Spilling *natural* freedom, seeking *natural* wild.

Soft suggesting Serena

White headed Elaine

Sharp dressed men's glasses hiding their shame

Soft style uninspired

White hints at the pain

Shield the bad from the rivers, from the mountains, from the rain.

Knowing the high notes like knowing your face
Ashamed to sing along
Rather wash windows in silence than speak through the haze
Tell me your favorite song
One you refuse to sing alone
Please
Too ashamed when you sing along.
Guiding my hand through the dark parts of my days
Past abstract sense of wrong
Knowing all around me before feeling my embrace
Teach me, tell me I'm strong
Kiss me, dye my hair blonde
Please
Kill me when I lead you on.
All knowing lips held in everlasting refrain
Encompassing your exact change and unshared birthdays
All knowing love of unremarkable shame
Engrossed in the parks and the fields brown and plain
The end of my day
Kiss me and I'll be the same.

Sheets of security stripped in coming freedoms
Starlit dorm rooms . I can buy my own shoes
First alone point of view . First good morning empty room
A choice of church on either side of the street
Sheets of security before life goes discreet.
Darkening indecency from stark stringent teens
Intellectual obesity . Borrowed words from a hollow man
Fluctuating insecurity . Filed out from wine and grams
Sheets of stripped security to find out who I am.
Days spent showering gifts on Sara
Bought smile alleviates fear
Days spent throning my own persona
Chiding brothers age and disappear.
Nights purchase muting mindset
Dim when sunlight clears
Nights spent looking for meaningful reset
Engraving scars into my peers.
Sheets of security stripped in coming kingdoms
Stripped of all sanctity I bury what was once clear
A bargain for living without any distinctions
Binding my stability . Constricting my passion.

The optimist struggles with that clouded reprieve, the prison sentence death penalty

watching while goals turn to greed

While the wisemen want a ransom

While their world turns to green.

Dr. Destruction's daughter just wants to be seen, the sins of her father gleam in a cryptic kind of mean

Dr. Destruction's daughter left home for the seas

Dr. Destruction's daughter strung up in the trees.

Never to be a martyr, never to unsee what she'd seen

Never to revolt at a father, to be more than a queen

Dr. Destruction's daughter attempting to flee

Nowhere to run when frustration burst at its seams.

The realist struggles to console their own precise prophecy, the bittersweet fruits

reluctantly picked from the vine

No joy in ardent warning

Never wanting to read the signs

Dr. Destruction's daughter left to face masses of greed

Dr. Destruction's daughter strung up in a tree.

Gracious man living

I believe motherhood as truth

Of greed's backseat to healing

Of the brotherhood of youth

Of Dr. Destruction and of his lost daughter

He wept while seeing fatal proof.

Fall from behind and trust that you'll find
A place inside my arms
A lover's reply and a lovelorn goodbye
A march beyond your charm
I've gotten lazy
But I'm looking for you tonight.
When starlight arrives and the wind washes by
When Main St. river's gleam
You hire a sign and stage when you'll cry
You hate when I tell you my dreams
I think you've gone crazy
But you sigh yourself to sleep at night.
You keeping score of who has loved who more
You and your time keeper's eye
You count the time between bereft and goodbye
This story's played out in your mind
I see the sky's getting hazy
Let's return to our youth tonight.
Shivering leaves
Child-like beliefs
Healing and being held
Vivid new scenes
Winter-like dreams
Alone when the storm starts to swell
Wind howling like Daisy
I hope it shakes skyscrapers to hell
Wind howling, I'm lazy
I promised that I'd never tell.

A needless supply of feeling that I found inside Angelo's bag
On a day when the supplemental healing found more than my sympathetic demerit of
the drab
The day when the effort met meaning
Before I snuck through Angelo's bag.
A godlike sense of truth seeking
Soon I sensed what Angelo lacked
His power in clarity of feeling
And desperation to give it all back.
A shameless supply of his kneeling, Angelo's apology for times that he cracked
The guard sanctions sanitized feeling
The bars give me times I want back.
Angelo's brother moved far away when the boy came bumbling back
Angelo bought me a dictionary
Told me "write or my eyes turn to black!"
Angelo left me his sanctuary
Pen ink spills from the things that we lack.
You're charming you're able you speak unlike the voices I've heard
A far cry from stable, you guided me along all new shores
But this charmer's unable
His guises crumble all my words
His guises splitting him in thirds
His guises walk away unsure
Sanctum of words.
Should I see morning's light? It's covered by the coat we share
I might stay late tonight, but you can't promise me who will appear
This charmer's approaching
He walks away to disappear
This charmer's invoking
A primer to a fall far from here
Angelo's paralysis fear.

Do you remember kissing the writer
In the dark that reminds him
Of the time when his shoulders gave
Way, commit new strength to guide him.
Do you remember screaming out
His name and so many attempts to tie him
To the shackles of a future's
Vagary, contempt for lying.
Do you say you found someone
Who calls back when you try him
Or do you say you kissed a writer
Turned to a fly and sensed his crying
Are you honest when he laughs and
Are you patient in this speech
Do they think you got a lot from me and
Have I caught you a love
So sweet?
Vagary. The narcissist and themselves
Obscurity. A purgatory worse than hell
You lie to your friends and the family you tell
Kissing a writer. Sneaking under his shell.

Old organs in the distance
A time you walked me through the snow
Garfunkel's *Kathy* singing
April front row I'm at the show
Depraved dalliancing, the price you pay to sleep alone
And I'm still double dipping, you show me where you want to go.
You're rancid in your winning
You start to smell just like the dough
You're sacrifice is burning
You try anything to take me home.
Did you try to pick up my
Feet when you walked me through the snow?
Did you buy me a seat or
Would you have ditched me at your show?
I'll guide my own deception, you
Instill this resurrection, don't
Call me when you make it home.
Old organs in the distance
Cold breath fogged up the lies you wrote
Old organs on the church steps
Just don't you dare leave me alone.

You walked along the beach and listed favorite spots to go. Rebecca's peak, Becca's
tavern, Becca's skate and Becca's bowl.
You talked around me towards the things that mattered. Rebecca's loving eyes for Mr.
Vincent Van Gogh.

Gold Dust Woman

Boxes of wine

Dollar Store rice pudding

Charcoal underneath flames.

Bare feet cracked shells along Washington beach. Rebecca's speeches turned into her
crimes.

You bled out times that you fell to your knees. Rebecca's secrets, Becca's stealing,
Becca's affinity to lie.

Wanted from Miami

To New York

Through gardens of time

From Pittsburgh

To Philly

Into this heart of mine.

You caught my lie in 1995. you

Left without sparing my goodbye. he

Picked you up from

That trip through the sky. you

Send me something that I won't describe. it

Caught me looking back in time. when

Arms weren't so heavy

Skin not so dry. you

Brought me children

To extend my time. you

Lived for instants

Whatever felt sublime. I

Couldn't stop time. 1995. I'm

Maladjusted. chose a life of crime. the

Boys don't know me. only remaining time. I

Said I would love you 'til the day I die. it

Shouldn't be so lonely on the day I die

When I figure my way back in time. I

Flick a lighter

See the sign

A new September

1995.

A cut from my perception
From my gut to my reception
Through my eyes. A resurrection
To despise the insurrection. Through my eyes
Bisecting the connection
To dissect "noble" professions
To leave my mind before confessions
From getting high on truth's deflection
To bide my time away from reverence.
A cut above my eye and another below my belt
Becca Lambier's blotting fingers heartfelt
Stinging under skin. The nails tear through my shields
The wounded fall prey. Revering claws of the healed.
A cut above her faith in me
The rut of hiding what's blessed
She seeks the sky while she's scraping me
Becca's God of beautiful disconnect
Vengeful God is beautifully incorrect.

What I'm seeking, everlasting sun of shared language

That waking state of seduction

That attention in the mines of distraction.

What I'm seeking, evacuate anxiety in a touch of my hand

The breathing, the sinking, the ventures into new lands

That synchronization, our bleeding in vows, practiced lines

That wakeful addiction to the crutch of my life

That spinning rendition

Mimicking highlights of strife.

My skin

My eyes

They're peeling

My scramble escapes the light

The things I say I'm seeking

My darkening lack of might.

Splintered oak burns into kindling, you try to suck my air

Your father and the bones that are showing, you're checking your hair in the mirror.

A check won't mean one thing to soft hands

The doors flinging open

You've done nothing but lie

The father, the son, immaculate deny

The corners that cut the unspoken

The dollar game, irrational child.

Splintering oak burning bridges, morality's selective revival

The blind people call for repealing, the cardholders look on and smile.

Ignore a siren behind you

Shake off the crooked smiles

The father gave blinders to guide you

You win and you win and the smoke starts to pile

The dollar game, irrational child.

Seek the sycophants in town
Seek the scorn of dower Ben
The guiding motionless surround the Goddesses of all that's grim
Seek the love that's winding down
Find the darkness of desirable men.
The last was all but written down
The pen's run out again
Great walls of scribbling surrounds the tasteless paintings hung, a kin
To the sorry let me downs and that borrowing bastard name of Ben
Seek something more than the martyr
Find the darkness of desirable men.

There's a mole standing on top of the ground it could choose to dig in to

There's an eagle standing under skylines

The trees are growing out

But their roots stay planted

There's choice to stay with me tonight.

A guiding winged flight could have left me stranded

A dig away from what's bright can't be mine

But the mole braves the sun

The eagle has landed

There's choice to stay with me tonight.

This is

The virtuous fight for a life above the ground

The warm glow that shines on the brave who survive

The guardian mole and the vagabond eagle

The celebration of those that wake up and choose life.

Made in the USA
Coppell, TX
19 September 2021

62653764R00049